Standing Naked

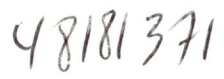

Standing Naked

❦

New and Selected Poems by

Jim Heynen

A JAMES R. HEPWORTH BOOK
CONFLUENCE PRESS, INC. • LEWISTON, IDAHO

ACKNOWLEDGEMENTS

Many of these poems appeared in the following collections, often in different form:
How The Sow Became A Goddess, Confluence Press (1977)
A Suitable Church, Copper Canyon Press (1981)

Other poems first appeared in the following publications:
"Tourist Guide: How You Can Tell For Sure When You're In South Dakota"
in *The South Dakota Review*
"I Think That I Shall Never See" in *Talking River Review*
"What Women Taught Me About Water" in *The Georgia Review*
"Atlantic Flyway" in *Place*
"Child Lost In Campus Coffee Shop" in *Poetry Northwest*
"Shortcomings" in *Memphis State Review*
"Sioux Center, Iowa" in *Idaho's Poetry: A Centennial Anthology* (1988)

For more information, please visit the author's website at www.jimheynen.com.

Publication of Confluence Press books is made possible, in part, by the generosity of the Idaho Commission on the Arts, Lewis-Clark State College, and Washington State University.

© 2001 by Jim Heynen. All rights reserved.

No part of this book may be reproduced in any manner without the express written consent of the publisher, except in the case of brief excerpts in critical reviews and articles. All inquiries should be addressed to: Confluence Press, Inc., 500 Eighth Avenue, Lewiston, Idaho 83501. Website: www.confluencepress.com

Dustjacket design by A. E. Grey.
Book design by R. L. Watkins.

FIRST EDITION
10 9 8 7 6 5 4 3 2 1

ISBN: 1-881090-39-6

Published by:
Confluence Press, Inc.
Lewis-Clark State College
500 Eighth Avenue
Lewiston, ID 83501
(208) 799-2336

Distributed by:
Midwest Trade Books
1263 Southwest Boulevard
Kansas City, KS 66103
(913) 831-2233
Fax (913) 362-7401

Contents

3   Child Lost In Campus Coffee Shop
4   What Women Taught Me About Water
5   The Barn
6   Standing Naked Before The Woman
7   You Hate Cats?
8   Eternity
9   Valentine
10 Love Among the Escargot
12 On Civility
13 The Clean People
14 On Middle Age
16 Falling out of Love
17 Staying With Old People
18 Please. Take. The Ticket.
19 Airports
20 TOURIST GUIDE:
    How You Can Tell For Sure
    When You're in South Dakota
21 Atlantic Flyway
22 Miniature Golf
23 Morning Coffee
25 Shortcomings
26 Putting in a Window
27 Painting the House
28 I Think That I Shall Never See…
29 Conversation
30 Building A Cradle
32 Shall I Teach My Daughter to Fear the Ocean?
33 To Live With Children
34 There is no praise
35 Mother Listening
36 The Old Farmer Speaks of the Millenium
37 Iowa Poem
38 My Father, Still A Farmer

40　Our Farm/Our Family
41　Morning Chores
43　Rock Valley, Iowa
45　Sioux Center, Iowa
47　Snow Storm
48　The Man Who Sharpened Saws
50　The Great Strength
51　Kansas Farmer
54　Yellow Girl
56　Sunset
57　Farrowing Pen
59　During the First Three Minutes of Life
60　Sometimes A Sow
62　Tornado Alert

Child Lost In Campus Coffee Shop

In this peculiar place
a smile could be lust
or pleasure with a fact.
The hand that rises, nervous,
could go anywhere. It touches
down on page 424. And here comes
someone with banners of
reproach. Repent. Begin. Resolve.
A saucer clatters to the floor.
Brimming ashtrays. An ad for peace.
At every table disparity
nudges for its place.

Such times when anything
can be, the way the poem
may flare its tiny lungs
to breathe the disparate air,
a world conforms. So now,
like some determined animal
ruling night with sound,
the child's scream invades us.
Our faces, our whole lives turn.
We lean together, reluctant,
rearranged, and one.

What Women Taught Me About Water

They taught me to swim, but I was slow at it because a woman's arms and legs in water make it look so easy. You kick too hard, one woman told me. Trust the water, she said, it will hold you up. She showed me by lifting me level with the water, but I knew it was a woman's hands holding me up, not the water. I learned to trust a woman's hands, but not the water. Another woman said, Fill your lungs with air and you'll hardly have to do anything. She was right, but when I exhaled, deflated, I needed her to keep me from sinking. One woman said, Hold on to my shoulders and kick, I'll do the rest. I did this and stayed afloat beautifully, but I knew we made a bad picture, a woman carrying a man on her shoulders like that. Then one woman said, You're hopeless. Why don't you watch a dog and learn to dog-paddle? Which is what I did. So today when you see women swimming, look for me among them. I'm the one with the grateful eyes, head lolling slowly along the surface.

The Barn

It is like entering a barn,
coming close to you
as to a warm object
in a sheltered place,
like a farmer with cold hands
to the heat of a steady flank.
The secrets that throb
in the steaming walls of a barn
are like our love
out of control
skittering through hay,
harmless and filled
with unobserved joy.

I smile now
as I smile at motorists
who speed past barns pointing
Look! Look!
to the silhouettes of barns
but who have never entered a cave
or heard their secrets echo
between rafters of a barn!

I think we are building a barn
or the reason for barns:
the black sow
half-hidden behind your skirt,
the quiet grunting
goddess of pleasure,
this renewable haven
of straw and unrefined musk.

Standing Naked Before The Woman

At noon in broad, over-exposing daylight, fresh from
mid-day love, his leisurely flesh shines for her, still flushed
with her agile praise. Not in pompous glory in these
golden, ripening middle years when the skin is flavored
with wise wrinkles and bold bulges shaped for reclining,
nor in the brazen manner of conquest, a knight at the gate,
nor a servant of purloined pleasure, a thief of delight,
but sanctified wholly, unencumberedly, totally, with no
due credit, with few fleshly credentials, a no-deposit/no-return
man of the noon-day sun. He knows the real light
is hers. Old memories of old loves scatter like scared rodents
found out by the bright light of her persistent, her sculpting
eyes, so long and pleasurable, so forgiving and fragrant
with sustained desire that he can only accept this dream:
to be reborn at midday in the full-orbed eyes of a generous
woman.

You Hate Cats?

But I like the cat in you,
the way the keen claws of you
nestle in the fur and purr of you.

I like your slim cat limbs
and tongue. I like the way
you see and find me in the dark.

I like the way you stalk me,
and how you pounce, and how
you throw me in the air,

and how you shed and spread
your smell across my lips,
then lick me clean.

Eternity

They lie in bed talking foolishly
about eternity. "Just remember,"
he says, "there is as much eternity
behind us as ahead of us."
"I don't like this kind of talk,"
she says, and rolls over, silent.

A little later he starts up again
about eternity. "Get off it," she says.
"We have better things to do with our time
than waste it on eternity."
"Good point," he says,
though it is too late to start over.

Valentine

Among maple leaves in winter, you're the one that doesn't fall.
Among owls, you are the one awake at noon.
Among birds, you are the cardinal on the chimney.
Among fish, you are the one who ignores the bait.

Among lunches, you are the free one.
Among dinners, you are a full course.
Among carrots, you are the horses' favorite.
Among mittens, you are Icelandic wool.

Among the counters, you are numberless.
Among virtues, you are Madam Generous.
Among the self-righteous, you are the skeptic.
In the marts of commerce, you are the boutique.

Among tables, you are the one with lace napkins.
Among chairs, you are the sturdy wing-back.
Among carpenter ants, you are the major worker.
Among rugs, you are the spotless one.

Among sheep, you're the one who won't follow,
among pheasants, the one who won't flush.
But among bears, you're the one dancing
around the fire in the forest of my heart.

Love Among the Escargot

Ou as tu appris a manger des escargot ca?

At eight a.m. I go to clip
oregano for eggs, then
watch the escargot
slide toward each other's scent,
exploring with antennae
like cautious hands.

I've read about these lovers
and now here they are:
from lips like camels',
voluptuous and soft,
they extend tongues armed
with tiny spears, which
gently used arouse their necks
to bluish white.

Now one bites
and sends its partner
ebbing to its shell,
regaining courage there
to reconnect. I know
their genitals
are hidden until they're ready,
resting behind the right,
the glinting, eye.
They see what they are doing.
Escargot move slow,
these wavy snails,
two hours trembling
through morning traffic,
extending and retreating,
their arched forms transfixed

in sexual politics. Hermaphroditic,
they stand on equal ground,
flinging spermy darts
called cupid's arrows.

I hold my breath, lean down
to watch: lip-locked,
they dodge and dance,
prolonging love by not being hit,
their arrows wavering
in air like second thoughts.
When they have pierced,
they glide away
on their own slow tide,
maneuvering as always
the spiral of themselves,
centered, through a world of green.
My hunger gone,
I feel no loss.
It is almost noon.

On Civility

When you get older,
making new friends
is not easy, especially for
men. I know. Women

are easier, with each other,
and with us. Younger women,
too, make friends easily—
because they trust us, think
we don't think of sex
with them. Which, of course,
is not true. But our civility
protects us, and them. Pretense,
yes, but the pretense of civility
is not pretense, it is
civility. Civility, like thick
ice on a Minnesota lake,
keeps the lonely old
fisherman safe.

The Clean People

The clean people worry me.
Wherever I go, I face the glare
of their immaculate smiles,
their polished demeanor
declaring the good life of order.
Where is the smudged
message of grief,
the scuff-marks of pain?
With all the dirt in the world,
who got theirs?

I think I am one
and take my place with the soiled.
We are the others
who cannot balance budgets,
nor wear white to our weddings.
Our garb is the haggard
will to survive.
Our language is the mono-
syllabics of dust.
Disorderly, vagrant,
we make our salacious way,
staining the world as we go.
We sing of flesh and the earth,
while they,
haloed in an absence of filth
must live near God,
their heavenly songs
lodged in the unmarred
keyboards of their grins.

Here they come now,
their clean mouths open,
spilling light as they go.

On Middle Age

I have been thinking about red flowers
and how the sight and thought of beauty
makes your blue eyes sparkle.
I have been thinking about color and loss,
about how all that is lovely and living must grow,
bloom, ripen in its color, and diminish.

I watch the golden fields diminish
in their flourishing. The flowers,
joyous in their colors, grow
beyond exuberant and glorious beauty,
as if celebrating the approach of inevitable loss.
Is it the blessing or curse of life to sparkle

at the height of its passing? Do we sparkle
like stars whose light does not diminish
when they are gone? Is loss
but the last bloom of the most lovely flowers,
the culmination and afterglow of beauty?
Even now as you and I grow

older, there is joy in our new colors. We grow
lighter against darkness, like the stars sparkling,
a bright and lingering beauty
that does not diminish
quickly like the sudden flourish and fall of flowers.
We go with a gradual grace whose loss

would be harsher than losing former colors. No loss
is greater than in that which no longer grows,
bending and wavering, but has hardened like plastic flowers,
lifeless and gathering dust, which cannot sparkle
in its going and cannot diminish,
never having known the living pain of beauty.

I have been thinking about beauty.
I have been thinking about loss.
I have been thinking about you who do not diminish
in color and grace as you grow.
Even now your blue eyes sparkle
as you gather the season's last flowers.

I accept the loss that comes as we grow
toward our fullest beauty. May we still sparkle
as the seasons diminish our favorite passing flowers.

Falling out of Love

Let it be like balding.
Not the daily loss
that seems to be everywhere,
clogging your drain, sticking
to your comb or tooth brush,
staying in bed with your pillow
while you rise, less whole,
to confront the growing absence.

Let it be like balding,
like the moon rising through the forest,
a slow ascent into the night
you find yourself alone,
whole, declaring
a crisp October sky.

Staying With Old People

I knew I'd like them
when I saw their old
black car—its long

gentle dents said
something about kindness,
about how to meet

an adversary. Do you
suppose the greatest
kindness is thoughtless?

He gets up early
and makes tea. He takes
his false teeth from

a glass and refills it
with warm water. Her teeth
are still in there,

warming up. When she
comes, those warm
teeth slide

into her warm mouth
so easily she hardly
notices her own smile.

Please. Take. The Ticket.

The spell of her voice
as I drive into the airport
short-term parking lot.

Please. Take. The ticket.
I sense her urgency,
the tension,

as she emits each
word before mouthing
the next.

For you, my Mystery,
I will. I say,
Yes, I say.

Thank you,
I say. Thank you
so very much.

I drive on with the slight
metallic scent of her
on the blue ticket,

the image of her
sad dark eyes, her
dry lips.

Behind me
I hear her plaintive voice
to the next drivers.

Please. Take. The Ticket.
Please. Take. The Ticket.
Please. Take. The Ticket.

Airports

I love the anonymity of airports,
the confusion of luggage and faces.

I love the indifference of Muzak
following from car park to terminal.

I love the flashing credit cards,
the indistinguishable fixing of signatures.

I love the impersonal computers
charting our lives in light waves.

I love the predictable gift shops,
the recurring rare turquoise and coral.

I love the metal detectors,
the televised shadows of shave cream.

I love the uniformed flight crew.
I love their uniform smiles.

I love the hydraulic ramps
attaching to the planes like parasites.

I love keeping step with my neighbors
as we silently march in together

and slide off in our numbered places
into the far dispassionate sky.

TOURIST GUIDE:
How You Can Tell For Sure When You're in South Dakota

You drive down Main Street
of the first town you come to.

There's a traffic light.
Always. Prestige.

When it sees you coming,
it turns red.

You stop and you're exposed,
and you know it.

A thin cowboy's rabid dog
eyes you from the pool hall.

Then a thick old man
thumps down from the curb.

He's in front of your car
when the light turns green.

Something slow meets your eye.
An eye meets your eye.

You smile.
It doesn't.

You start to drive away.
The whole world stalls.

Atlantic Flyway

Over Virginia,
fifty miles
from the Atlantic,
a flock of snow geese
stalls out. The high
loosely knit V
sways like a mobile.

Last year
what guided them in—
the woods, the short
Mennonite steeple?
Now nests
are basketball nets
dangling from garages
and the small
channels of water
are roads
feeding into themselves
again and again.

The survivors
hold, treading air.
Their necks
like forefingers
beckon the ocean
to come in and greet them.
Or is this all:
wings of desire,
throats that chant
now now now?

Miniature Golf

Their whole lives have led to this.
In 1955 they turned on
their big TVs to shrink
farther into their stuffed chairs.
In 1960 they were swallowed
by huge shark-tailed cars
but survived like little Jonahs.
In the 80s they found the malls
so large they were but gumdrops
on the sleek corridors.
For decades they have persisted,
determined in their diminution:
houses of such abundant floor space
they got lost in the shag;
DC 10s on whose grand bodies
they clung like fleas
on the backs of majestic Grizzlies.
Look at them now.
These tiny people drive about
in compact cars no bigger
than what is left of their lives.
Arriving here, they smile
through mouths grown small
as cordial glasses. Somehow,
they seem grandly happy.
Mother delivers a good one
down the ten-foot fairway.
And look at grandpa smack
that ball across the two-foot pond!
What's my score? shouts father
at the 9th hole. One less than
last time! he shouts. One less!
One less! One less!

Morning Coffee

A terribly plain woman
takes the next booth.
Her hair is spaghetti on her cheeks,
her face a bowl of milk.
When she sheds her faded coat,
the dead sleeves slump to the floor.
What remains is a bland
encounter with space, the faint
odor of bread dough.

Still, something intrigues me.
My urge is to lead her to color, through
prisms of joy, rainbows of delight.
Come with me, says the kaleidoscope of my eyes,
I am the evangelist of lipstick and rouge.

Is every miracle a joke? I wonder,
thinking back on that morning, when,
not her eyes, but my eyes
were opened. As she listlessly lifted
her cup to her lips,
her gray blouse tightened
and I saw
a flash of extravagant color.
As if struck on the brow,
I saw red, I saw flowers, I saw blue,
I saw clowns and three-dimensional balloons.
As in an instant we might see
the bright gill of a trout in stale water—
a whole world was changed!

Even now
I do not know what it was in the V
where her blouse met her breasts,
whether a fringe of brassier,

or birthmark,
or a glamorous tattoo.
I only remember that miniature
Mardi Gras of color
in whatever the plain lady wore on her heart.

Then, as easily as an arm
returns to a table,
it was gone.
Again, the waters were gray,
but I know,
as a few people know
what moves in the depths of Loch Ness,
that the plain woman breathes with a secret
so dazzling she is saving us from it.

Is it only a wish, her hidden
desire to be free?
No, the color is all, the rest
a disguise.
Believe me,
if you see,
as if through a cloud,
this woman you mistake for a yawn,
beware. Be calm.
If ever she thought we knew,
the sea of her passion would devour us.

Shortcomings

We are the little
black holes of your life,
negative and capable
of being more than you are.
       *   *

You want to be loved
for your beauty
or strength.
We will enter you
through your weakest link.
       *   *

We are the only part
of your life that comes easy.
       *   *

On the farm
the windmill whirled
through the night.
While the supply tank
flooded, animals drank
from your neglect.
       *   *

Everyone watched
to see what he would do wrong
next. When he did nothing
wrong, friends, audience,
and lovers left him.
       *   *

Truly, a person
is like a balloon.
If you squeeze the air out
in one place,
it appears in another.

Putting in a Window

Who would have thought
behind that wall
was a garden!
What I have watered and touched—
the forsythia, magnolia,
azaleas and forget-me-nots;
the rhododendron, roses, and lilacs,
the carrots! Now I see through my window
the garden as I once saw my lover
through the eyes of a stranger who desired her.
The weeds fade like the clutter of clothing
as I see through my window a rebirth of beauty,
an unspoiled garden.

Beside me the section of wall
is all that I wish undone
fallen out of my life.
My old self fades in the sawdust
as I open myself to my window.
I have opened the world with my window!

And what can I give you, contained
on this surface? The wish that you too
may open. The possibility, the clarity
of window, the song
that is hiding in silence.

Painting the House

– dedicated to the students who bartered a house painting for a writing class

Let's shadow-paint the house!
No brushes, no paint,
we'll spread our shadows across the peeling boards!
Follow your unlit side to work.
We have until sunset.

You with the tiny hands,
shadow-paint the trim.
You with the big hips,
your work is outlined already.
You with the lofty ideas,
the gables are yours.
You two who would mix romance with work,
let no light come between you.

May this be work of the spirit, not a job
but a process, like the poem
of your life, starting at the top and working
down, covering mistakes as you go.
You can start anywhere, the way the new
life starts where it wants, perhaps at the center.
Let what you are happen. Move on.
Your choices will narrow as you go
until it is no longer your will but the small
space calling you home.

I Think That I Shall Never See...

> "Seeing a tree as a praying figure is somewhat hackneyed."
> – *from a poetry textbook*

I know what I see:
The blue spruce outside my window
kneels for morning prayers.
Meanwhile, the oak across the street
scratches the back of the tired sky
and a small bush next door
embraces the innocent sparrow.

And I know what I know:
how the seasons forgive and
restore the dormant and listless:
butterfly, moth, scorpion, insatiable
medfly, militant hornet, who knows what.

Let's face it: everything needs help.
Even this cocoon where my mind
takes solace in its barky recesses
can feel the reverent trees' new breath.
Any second now: exultant branches!
a choir of leaves! O!

Conversation

Through the sound of leaf-
blowers, sirens, engine chatter,

comes the other persistent
conversation: sparrows at

love-play along the boulevard,
the half-tailed squirrel still

squirreling around trees, hedging
its bets against inflation,

and the ubiquitous crows,
inky punctuation marks

on the run-on neighborhood,
harassed now by cacophonous

starlings and the blue jay
splashing empty the neighbor's

bird-bath. The parts fitting. A
blue heron anchored against

the sky with jet trails farther
up. The dogs at their eye-level

seeing only each other.
What a world! This

busyness, the steady counter-
pointing, like a subscript, like a lecture

playing in the background, or the real
program punching through commercials.

Building A Cradle

~ for fathers

In the fourth month
when the quickening spreads
into your limbs,
take a walk in the woods.
Find the stump
in whose open mouth
a seed has taken root.
Do not disturb it.

In the fifth month
return to the forest
through the confusion
of things fallen
or growing, find the log
that lies nervously
in its hollow.
Coax it
until it follows you home.

In the sixth month
linger long with the woman.
Study the grain of her skin.
Let the lines become magnets in your mind
tugging toward alignment.

In the seventh month
watch the hands and feet
working from inside.
There's the carpenter!
Like an apprentice,
follow these movements
until they are yours.

In the eighth month
hold your hand on the taut
navel of the woman,
then on the wood.
Follow the life force in,
working slowly with what tools you have,
whittling, shaping with a lathe,
with your fingers,
with your tongue.

During the ninth month
when distinctions blur
between you, the woman,
the stranger, and the wood,
do not argue with the shape
as it forms,
don't look back,
let it go!
That morning you find it
rocking by itself,
it is finished.

Shall I Teach My Daughter to Fear the Ocean?

To her
beauty is gentle,
the surf, the churning undertow—
all smooth forms one
with breast or hand. Her eyes
float out and she, toddling,
buoyed by wonder, would embrace
the sea. The magic stones
light up the tide,
the slow boats gliding
call Emily. I too hear
the foghorns, sirens
to the deep. My voice
is danger, a calling
to knowledge
of gasp and fall.
Though I wish to walk with you
there avid as Christ
for a surface firm
and warm beneath us,
I will show you
this life, a constant
recoil of desire.
My hand on your shoulder
is the first denial.
I am teaching my daughter
to fear the ocean.

To Live With Children

We fix our rocky memories
against their fluid minds.
We resist them yet listen,
trying not to hear old echoes.
Then one says,
The tooth fairy is a white spider.
Then one says,
Your nose is so long
it can smell dinosaur bones.
How are we to survive our resurrection?
Age is focus
but they disperse. The orgy
of their eating. The diffusion of food.
One puts a banana in his mouth
and pulls out a pineapple.
The tablecloth sprouts sprouts.
They scatter our tidy world with laughter.
The children grow hair and teeth,
grow legs, grow arms, shed hair,
grow more, shed teeth, grow more.
The children have so many teeth!
And their eyes! Their eyes!
They shatter our world
with their seeing!

There is no praise

excels the moment of caring.
In stooping I praise,
without knowing, my son,
seven, feverish and weak,
face down in his pillow.
I do not remember the arms
lifting me in my sickness.
I do not remember the fevers,
though I bend to his body quivering
and helpless, wipe the face
clean, give him water to rinse,
and know a circle is closing.
I am selfish and driven
in the manner of planets,
this slow, impersonal act,
this heavy tide,
this plant in its seasonal growth.
I wait for the fever to break,
though I do not feel the care of my caring.
His warm hand touches my neck
like a vine entwining a tree,
perhaps like a root
that is holding me steady.

Mother Listening

He is thirteen and the thin
feminine note in his voice breaks,
shatters and is lost in his dark
throat like a growl, a false tune
coming from a dark caged part
of himself, so that even *yes*
sounds like *no* now, and his
soft eyebrows look firmer over
the sound breaking through his
lips. Everything, even his walk,
more a defiant gait now,
builds around that grating voice.
No girl will have such a budding
monster, will she? Surely, others
of his kind will bruise him
back into himself, send him
kneeling back to the tender
boy who was my son. Who
was. Who was. Who was.

The Old Farmer Speaks of the Millennium

I told you this would happen.
The blind have led the blind
to a dead end.
We could lose everything.
We should have known better.
Let's face it, we've had it.
We're scraping the bottom of the barrel.
Our goose is cooked.
There's nowhere to go from here.
We're ruined.
There's no sense talking about it.
We've bought the big one.
We're a dead duck.
We've hit rock bottom.
We're done for.
Where were you?
Barking up the wrong tree?
Ignoring the handwriting on the wall?
Why did you let things get out of hand?
Too busy seizing the moment?
Too busy making hay?
Now look at us.
Up the creek without a paddle.
The verdict is in.
Our ship is sunk.
The jig is up.
Why didn't you do something?
Our backs are up against the wall.
The situation is beyond repair.
There's no sense talking about it.
I was right, wasn't I?
The prognosis is not good.

Iowa Poem

– Winter, Oregon

Winter, and father writes
from our white farm in Iowa,
How's the weather out there?
Have you found a suitable church?

What can I say?
The weather, father, it rains.
The grass is unnaturally green
and everyone's sick with the flu.
All this water
without any corn to drink it—
it all goes to waste in the sea.
But the weeds go on growing
and our soles rot from our feet.
Of course, there aren't any churches.
I've been out with umbrella searching
but the sky's too dark for steeples.

Father, let me say, Don't worry.
We'll all be all right, here or there.
In my hands there still lives a farmer
pulling weeds from this barren wet earth;
in my chest there's still a believer
praying for a clear cold sky.

My Father, Still A Farmer

My father, still a farmer
at sixty-two, wears overalls
like they used to—stripes,
bronze buttons to light a match on,
bib pockets for nails
or scribbled notes with cattle prices.
Still comes from the outhouse
with his suspenders buttoned wrong,
prefers this accident to belts
which give him stomach aches
and don't let in the air from the side
where you need it
on those hot sultry days.

At night in slippers
and wool pants
he's only half the man.
It makes me want to know
about the overalls. Something
about the overalls.
It's when he's in
those overalls I've seen his old arms
spring like willow limbs
to take a sick sow by the ears
and set her up,
or hay bales leaping shoulder high
as if they know he wants them there.

I know old cowboys ride good horses
and old hunters have good dogs,
but farmers never show their age
in such dependent ways. This is
a special secret, their way of getting on.
At night I'm left to wonder

at those limp and wrinkled stripes
hanging on the porch.
The strange and aged look,
implicit strength,
of old and idle men and things
waiting to become one.

Our Farm/Our Family

Land there in Iowa lay so flat
we never dared run naked through the fields
and only joked of swimming nude
in the creek so close to the railroad.
Now and then we did pee in the clover
but only on dark nights when the neighbors
were inside with their four-cornered eyes.

All roads there were straight,
barns rode the horizon like ships,
the sun was hours in setting,
and on the heaviest summer nights
a laugh could be heard for a mile.
We learned to be cautious as that albino fox
the whole township hunted for years.

So we were never exposed
except to ourselves on Saturday nights
when, just after eight, our family of five
conspired in the dim-lit kitchen,
stark-naked around the galvanized tub.
We laughed and pinched and took turns
scrubbing and using the same water.

Sunday morning the wide church pews
were our final test. We passed: father,
brother, and I in our black suits and starched collars;
mother, tightened in her corset, black hat and veil;
sister, too fully developed, draped in her loose
brassiere and the dress that kept everything private.
We liked things this way: the inside, the out.

Morning Chores

In his bed he turns toward light
and the odor of work on his hands,
toward the moist clothes on the floor
with the barnyard still breathing in them.
Outside the chorus begins:
roosters crowing, dogs barking,
but he is not sure of the dawn
until he hears himself calling the cows.
Dew collects on his shoes,
pigs rise from wet earth,
milk drips from the udders of cows.
Everywhere the fresh urge of morning
leads him into his story.
The cows eat from his hands,
the milk flows from his hands.
What happens between he doesn't know
and doesn't care. It is enough.

Now all he hears is that memory
as he rises in suburban light,
knowing too well he is here:
his hands full of dishes, a bed
with two cats and a wife
whose love sinks with him in yearning
for the small voice they both left bawling
in one lost field or another.

Still the residing light
for those who have lived among animals
is like a religion that stands
when the old church crumbles.
For to have moved with the beasts who know
more than reason or law
but who accept the sun in the morning
and the hands that feed them

is to have been the voice in a song
that no one was singing,
happier than those who praise
and know they are praising.
Even now he can feel
as the city untangles around him
that constant flow in the earth
that wants to be glad.

Rock Valley, Iowa

We farm boys came in droves
to the blinking red
on the water tower. That
wicked little town had girls
in tight pink jeans and smiles
too radiant to be pure, all
waiting at the roller rink,
who shivered when they heard
our muscles roll in our Levi's
as we eased from our polished black cars.

This is the story
of what never happens to farm boys
full of raunch and sweat,
swaggering through smells
of horse urine and ripe oats.
Oh, we tried, looked mean,
grinned from every sideline,
told dirty jokes, and laughed
in each other's eyes.
But our legs were thick:
we couldn't dance or sway
or stand on wheels.
Our hands
we couldn't trust
with strum or touch.
We didn't have a chance.

The girls
did what they could,
twisting by and smiling
at where we stood.
We couldn't move. While the
town boys, loose and slouchy,
did figure-8s, and gathered

all that beauty
in their slender hands.

Next morning in the cow barn
we didn't forget our failure,
but while our forearms rippled, milking,
we found a sly kind of patience
and gathered many secrets in our palms
that someone somewhere someday
would be glad to learn about.

Sioux Center, Iowa

Home of the Christian smile.
Not a center for Sioux.
The Dutch. A sub-
culture of yahs. Calvin-
istic and clean. Deep
winters. Sustained
by corn and thick
Holsteins, creamy
grins, and providential
care. Straight
furrows surround
the town. No mote,
no dike to protect it.
Only the creamery and grain
elevator, the old hatchery,
truck stops and bristling
steeples.

Do you think the people are nice?
The people are not nice.
The people are right.
Do you think the people are clean?
The people are clean.

Pictures of lonely hands praying.
Pictures of large horses.
Mosquitoes and white lawn chairs.
Miniature German Shepherds
in back car windows, their eyes
blinking the turns.

Do you think the people like baseball?
The people like baseball.
Do you think the people love?
The people love what is right.

John Deere and snowmobiles
and predestination for those
whom it hurts. Polished saddles.
Salads with whipped cream
and marshmallows. Thick
steaks.

Do you think the young people
drive in circles with new cars?
The young people
drive in circles with new cars.
The young people drive in circles
with new cars until they are aroused.

The new cars stop near cornfields
and graveyards and rock
in their tracks.
Do you think the people know the Beautiful?
A daughter in a white gown
who can play the church organ.
Do you think the people drink whiskey?
The people drink whiskey
in the next county.
Do you think the people would like you?
The people would not like you. You
are not one of them. But you
are important
where you are. God
loves those
who stay in their place.

Snow Storm

It never surprised us,
no more than had there been thieves
shadowing the barns at midnight.
Something inside us was ready.

Holding shovels high like rifles,
we'd leap from an upstairs window,
land staggering like crows in the whiteness,
and make our one choice, to dig.

All day we'd work, father and sons
carving paths through the barnyard,
driven by strength that kept growing
until it was almost a madness.

We raged like fire in dry timber,
parting the snow with a vengeance,
as if any moment it would rise
and try to inhale us.

At dusk we'd look back on the paths
and see they were more than we needed,
broad indecent swathes
through the undulant white.

We'd walk through, three abreast,
thinking we'd almost found love
for whatever sent the snow
or for the snow itself—

for anything so large
that laid itself at our feet
and asked us in.

The Man Who Sharpened Saws

His old green truck with the cracked
windshield had a soft bump to it
as it stumbled down the drive,
but the man who sharpened saws
was cruel. He'd kick cats
or feed steel shavings to the chickens
if they bothered him. Usually
they didn't—we'd clear his way
of chickens and hide the cats.

More than cruel,
he was a communist.
Dad said that's how he really
made his money. So
we made him a song:
    Bumpity bumpity
      Here comes the commie
      In his old green Chevy.
No one asked him to come,
but when he did,
we brought our saws
and watched the sparks fly in a steady light
as he eased his file along the bending blades.
It was like soothing music to us,
the nearest we ever heard to a violin.

When he finished,
he charged a dollar.
Once he forgot even that.
And that's how we knew for sure
he was a communist,
that and his posters we always refused:
ones with pictures of men with shovels.
Dad said those posters replaced the cross.

I think, for him, they did.
Still, when he finished, the saws glistened
a pure sharpness, and we'd celebrate
his leaving by sawing wood. Any wood.
It all was butter to us then.

But by spring, when he was almost
off our minds, the saws got dull,
and we'd wonder about him.
Sometimes we sang
>   Bumpity bumpity
>   *Now* where's that commie
>   In his old green Chevy?

We lived by principles when I was a boy,
so one summer we thought of putting up a sign
to keep him away. And we would have
if we'd had a saw sharp enough to make the sign.

The Great Strength

Those who bulged from their shirts
like straw from tightly tied bales,
who won fist fights at the fair,
caught the greased pig, wrestled a steer,
were strong men of the plains.
But the great strength was private,
known only to old farmers
who could see the power
hidden in the face of a peddler
or farm hand, in the strangely shaped body,
pinched shoulders and spreading hips,
bent over like hybrid grain in the wind.

When the fields had been cleared,
when the last hay was stacked,
the last fence fixed,
when the cellar was sealed for winter,
always, there was the accident,
and he would be there
with jackknife or pliers or bare hands,
his strength coming out
from all its secret parts.
For a moment we knew:
a wagon set upright,
a hand pulled free from moving gears.
It was all in the wrists, or the legs,
or the eyes. Afterwards

there was no excitement at all,
and only a few saw him fade back to his body.

Kansas Farmer

*"In good years it's so good
you don't want to leave;
in bad years it's so bad
you can't."*

This year it's good.
The rains come early
and settle in. All summer long
a heavy sky. Who remembers the man
who wrote his name in blood
on parchment land? What matters
when the sky is full? The cow bags
sway like time that's standing still.
The oak tree shades the earth worms
and their world softens like the sky.
You soften too
and you don't care when alfalfa thickens
to a bed so soft it asks your teenage son
to love his neighbor.

    (Look at the
farmer's hands! His muddy finger-
prints are contoured fields! His eyes
are like the sky and, looking down,
he thinks these hands are God's.)

Rapture fills the creek in good years.
The creek flows through your veins.
You dream of flying and live believing
there's nothing in the world
that can't be blessed. You bless
the sky and every furrow, soil
or flesh. The thick air's full of lust.
You bless the water and the sun.
Listen—on warm nights you can hear

the green corn grow, the top leaves
moving faster than the minute-hand
on your watch. What's time
in good years? October, and you
stack your dead corn high
in yellow pyramids, your testament
to sky and green.
Already next year's dust
starts to color all you've done.

   * * *

The bad year opens with a smile.
More birds than ever
stop to taste your soil. You
taste it too, first with fingers,
then your tongue. It's spring.
Your joyful body aches
from making ready. The dawns
are huge and red. What do the morning
glories say when they quiver near the fence?
You bare your nostrils
to all that's going on
and smell the sweet perfume
of something false. The steady cows
come home with no dew on their backs.
Fear rises in your groin. You plant
your seed and call it faith.
The summer sun burns low.
The earth pulls tight. The dry air
smells so clean you sniff yourself
remembering the scent of semen
in sweet clover after rain.
Now the hot
south wind comes whirling
through your fields. The tenderest
crops are first to go. Enormous
locusts perch mid-air against the sun.
The one-time rain

makes the wheat get rusty—it paints your hands
in dry-blood dust. You curse the sky
and dream of fire. Fire it is
in bad years. The August clouds of dust
fill your barns like smoke. Horse nettle
lives on along the dry-bed creeks
and burns your wrists. The wasps
form packs of hate.
The whole world stings.
You clean your throat and spit wet earth
back against the burnished sky.
Now is the time to find
the deepest river of your soul.
You sit down on the porch,
close your eyes, and dig.

Yellow Girl

A young boy plays in the fields
around the pond. Often he imagines
when days are long with dust and sun
that he sees ducks and bullheads
swimming there.

But he knows the pond is dry.
He has been there, pinched the crawdads
into dust. He has gone there thirsty
hoping that a spring has broken loose
and water waves like oat fields in the breeze.

He waits for the great spring flood.
When it comes, for the first time he sees,
more than in dreams, water suspending
cornstalks from the trees like rotting fruit
and every field flowing with the flood.

When the plains emerge, he finds the pond
brimming with fresh, dark water,
and near the shore
a delicate and torn yellow dress
the flood has brought from somewhere.

He watches it move on waves,
wanting to reach and take it
but sees it live for water,
moving with the form
of a lovely girl swimming.

He has never learned to swim,
but he leaves his clothes
floating with hers on the water
where their sleeves reach to touch
like friendly fish or ducks.

He returns to his fields,
through the briars,
steps naked into the pasture
where he cannot find the yellow girl
nor imagine the fields where she lives.

Sunset

The cows
sink into the meadow,
small violet ships.
Pigs and their sticky night sounds
lie down together in their wallow.
The old dog,
smelling like all the animals,
follows silence from barn to barn.

Through the stillness
swallows carry the last light down
on thin wings of fire.
The red night.
The blue night.

A gray little whirlwind
stirs in the oat field.
Corn tassels tremble.
The cool north wind
sets me adrift.

Sounds of earth move me,
shadows of dreaming meadowlarks
move me. The air is alive
with the breath of animals.

Farrowing Pen

Last night
you snapped at my hand,
old bristly woman.
Now you ignore me,
don't even hear sparrows
chattering in the eaves.

Who could believe this—
the old sow with her frothy snout
shaping a dam out of straw,
mouthfuls of straw, each
edged into place for this
magnificent cradle,
this smooth-prowed boat,
this sow-nest!

It has only begun.
She falls in,
lies still as an egg
until contractions begin,
a breeze on a hedge,
bristles rippling, vagina
swelling and splitting with blood.
But still the ease,
slow commotion of birth.
The small pig arrives
and the sparrows never stop singing.

No one here is surprised,
not even the newborn
stepping out of its birth-sac,
the small ears unraveling
smooth as a conch
to hear its own life in straw,

the sparrows singing,
the sow's slow breathing.

Does she remember
the first task—
to straddle the umbilical cord,
break free and leave it
drying on the straw,
and to move on, circling the nest,
until the mouth, as now,
touches flesh,
and is home?

During the First Three Minutes of Life

The piglet
sucks

naps
wakes up

sniffs
the nipple next door

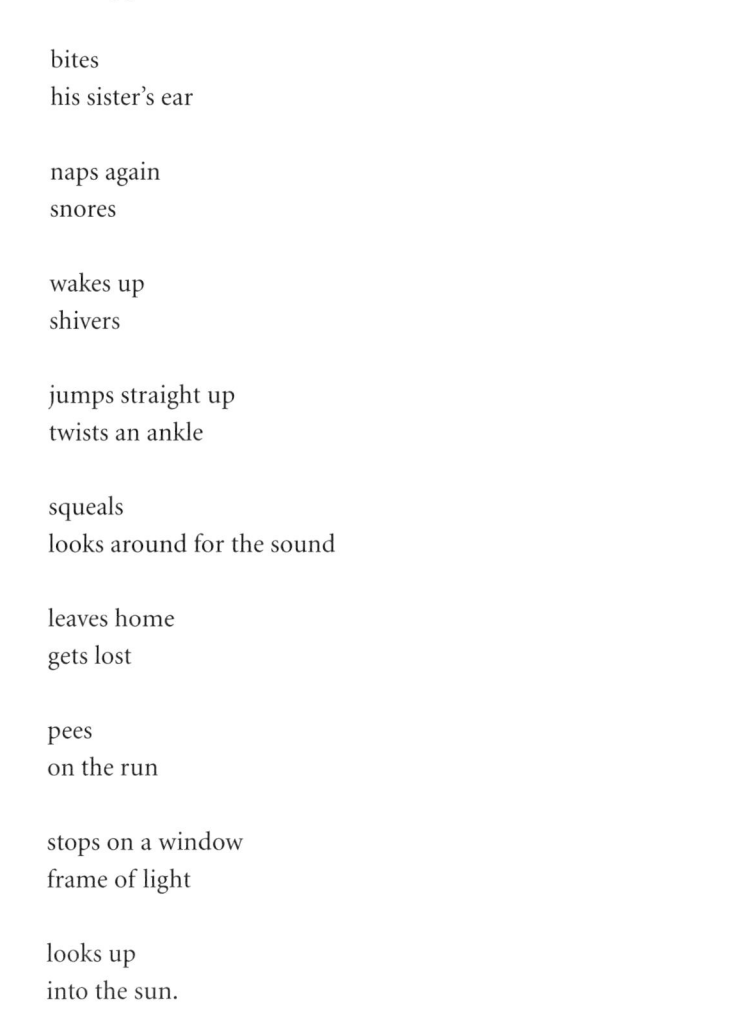

bites
his sister's ear

naps again
snores

wakes up
shivers

jumps straight up
twists an ankle

squeals
looks around for the sound

leaves home
gets lost

pees
on the run

stops on a window
frame of light

looks up
into the sun.

Sometimes A Sow

Sometimes a sow
couldn't have her young.
They'd catch
in the tight gate
of her womb
and she'd lie heaving
toward death.

When I was ten,
I learned a trick
to get them out—
a metal hook
in my hand
into the birth channel
shoulder deep
to find
the small snout.
I'd slip the hook
under the chin,
hold my breath
and pull.

Sometimes
the wishbone jaw
shattered
and the pig died,
but when it worked
the release was sudden—
a small form
wet in my hands.

At the sound of life
the sow would sigh
her jowled sigh

and I would sigh
and put the pig
bleeding
to her teats.

Tornado Alert

That night
against a copper sky there rose
a body, large and dark,
extending land to cloud.

On the dusty stack of last
year's hay I sat and watched it
lumber nearer, wavering, frayed,
and almost letting loose
to stringy clouds,
then tightening toward
human form. Steadily,
it looked at me,
and I knew it was a woman.

For all I knew of women
was there, the mystery I dreamed
beneath the flowing skirts of aunts,
the fleshy angles
of teen-age girls—
and now a broad hip
swaying, a lithesome
fluid rhythm
that was always foreign,
always close to my imagining—
a song translated to the sky
and one with it.

From all directions
came her silence breathing in
my breath, a feeling heavy
from inside that could have been
a wish to leap into
her grand revolving.

My hesitation broke
her silence into laughter,
shattering the oats.
I felt the urge the fence
posts followed leaping
from their dull lives in earth
to dance the sky,

or at least
to let my clothing go
the way the corn
in all its ordered rows
let go its leaves and seed to be
one with swirling cloud.

Half-mad with yearning,
half-crazed by fear,
I burrowed down to root myself
in hay. And then

from near the hog house
a sow ascended,
a wingless flight
into the guttural roar of mud and dust,
its thick form turning
slowly, its snout agape,
its short legs pedaling air—
a crazy celebration, her joining,
as if by choice, the sky
hilarious with debris.

First rain,
then the stinging sky,
struck my face.
All her darkness was upon me.
All her rage.

Standing Naked

The pig was gone.
I heard my own unwilling
scream of terror
and turned face-down, clawing
like a rodent trapped in hail.
With no choice but to live it out,
I scratched and writhed, prying
the stubborn sea
of hay, my only hope
a burial. Submerging
so deep that sight and sound
were gone,
I lived
the single smell
of molding, musty hay.

Whoever it was survived
climbed through my chest,
and I stood upright
into torrents of friendly rain
on the fire of torn skin.

The bristling sow
weaved through my mind.
Somewhere,
I imagined her
still skirmishing with filthy air,
still turning over and over
in a sky of wreckage.
I heard the rescue sirens,
frail strands of sound.
I saw the sad, disheveled farmyard.
I saw the waxen faces of my frightened
parents peering from the cellar.

And I laughed,
already denying those reports

of finding, thirty miles east,
stomach sliced by the free-wheeling
plowshares of the sky,
the haughty, grunting, earthy sow.

About the Author

Jim Heynen was born on a farm in northwest Iowa in one of the last areas of the state to get electricity. For his first eight years of education, he attended a one-room school house in Sioux County, Iowa, Welcome #3. He attended Calvin College and the University of Iowa. He received his M.F.A. in creative writing from the University of Oregon.

In addition to several collections of poetry, Heynen has published four collections of stories: *The One Room School House, You Know What Is Right, The Man Who Kept Cigars in His Cap,* and *The Boys' House: New & Selected Stories.* He has also published two novels for young adults, *Cosmos Coyote and William the Nice* and *Being Youngest.* Even more recently Heynen edited *Fishing for Chickens: Short Stories About Rural Youth.*

Since 1992 he has been Writer in Residence at St. Olaf College in Northfield, Minnesota. For more information on Jim Heynen and his work, visit www.jimheynen.com.

NORMANDALE COMMUNITY COLLEGE
LIBRARY
9700 FRANCE AVENUE SOUTH
BLOOMINGTON, MN 55431-4399